5155

TUNED DROVES

TUNED DROVES

Eric Baus

Octopus Books

Brooklyn, New York/Portland, Oregon

2008

Tuned Droves
©2008 Eric Baus

First Edition, 2008
ISBN: 978-0-9801938-1-7
Printed & bound in the USA

Cover design by Denny Schmickle
www.dennyschmickle.com

Octopus Books
Portland, Oregon & Brooklyn, New York
www.octopusbooks.net

for Sara Veglahn,
Noah Eli Gordon,
& Dorothea Lasky

ACKNOWLEDGMENTS

Thanks to the editors of 26, *Bridge, Cant, Coconut, Web Conjunctions, Crossroads, Crowd, Dislocate, foArm, Fascicle, Fourteen Hills, Glitterpony, LIT, The New Review of Literature, Skein, One Less, Octopus Magazine, Turnrow, Ur-Vox,* and *Weird Deer* for publishing versions of these poems. Portions of this book were published as the chapbook *Something Else The Music Was* (Braincase Press).

Contents

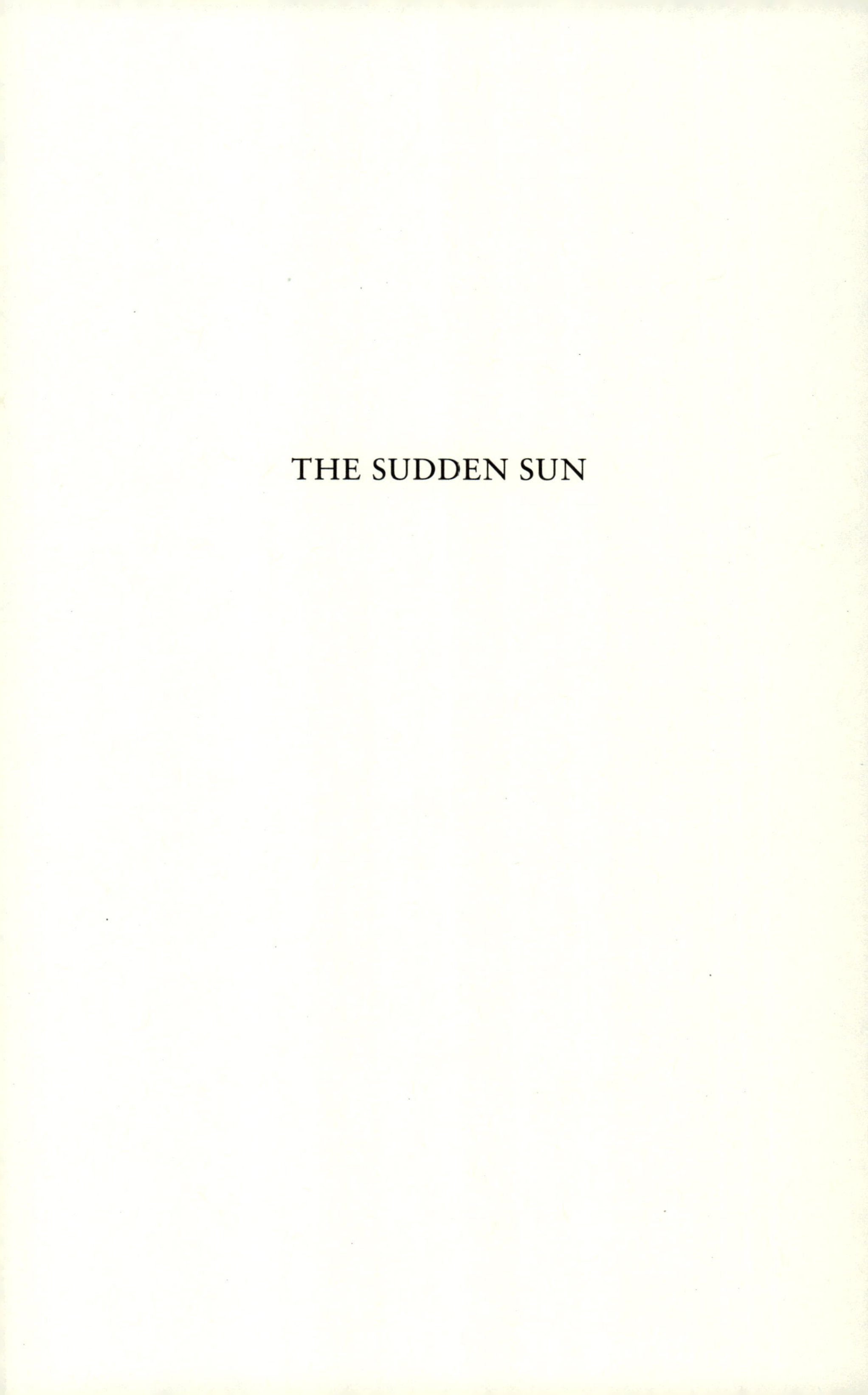

THE SUDDEN SUN

When a boy's mouth collapses into itself, tiny flames release from his limbs. Although this is a small flash, he is startled by the sudden sun.

SOMETHING ELSE THE MUSIC WAS

A woman leaves a bus and a man feels as if he has just stepped off of a train.

Rain is when you get wet is what he thinks next.

She thinks of orange when he is being quiet. Feeling red when she sees the sun.

Here her singing is speaking too. The sun is hot, I'm singing too.

The sun is orange, he says to himself.

•

The flames far away are red and red.

She sings her speech to me.

She says It is quiet. It begins on a bus. Rain is when red gets wet.

•

Her laugh is a reference to something she left. A paper reference, explains her laugh.

Like that, said a boy, a moment ago. I began like that man, in a tree.

Someone else's paper flowers. A particular climbing tree.

•

Birds feel red when it rains on a boy. They think "A boy is here."

He combs himself for pieces of snow.

It was almost nothing, he said.

•

She has seen the trick beginning with me trying to make a triangle with my fingers to show the distance between her, myself, and trying.

Her song was flickers or Variations on The Flicker.

She wants me to speak but I cannot begin anywhere I have not begun before.

For example, I begin to look around for the word lamp, and its echo, speaker.

I begin "A king without subjects."

I begin looking around, echoing places to make a triangle.

·

A boy gets a bird from cutting paper. Birds become themselves when he sees them.

Dear paper birds, I can always see you. A woman, a man, and paper birds.

What are you doing, paper bird?

Removing myself from the sky.

·

Her laugh is a word to compare to something. Her laugh is a word, explains the space.

A tree like that is where I am from.

When she does not eat a pomegranate she is making a reference.

I feel I am climbing a tree.

·

A woman writes a letter aloud.

She looks in her comb for small bits of hair, walking on seeds in the snow.

I am sorry it took me twenty pages to climb a tree is how she addresses herself.

I am writing so you will leave my title alone.

Leave my title alone.

I was not "I need your comb." She was the one who walked off a bus.

•

A woman explains to a boy the extra space around him lets small things disappear at night.

He feels as if he has just explained something by "The birds are feeling orange today."

A man is speaking to himself, leaving a bus.

A tree did nothing today.

•

She says my title is either A Variation on the Triangle or Variations for Triangle.

I am watching her face to decide.

Her laugh is a reference to another echo, paper speaking sun.

She wants me to speak but I cannot begin "A boy is getting lost."

•

I am sorry, a woman explains, but water birds aren't known for speaking.

She sings the distance she sees. A paper echo, beginner's water.

She wants me to speak but I cannot project. He walks like this, shows her voice.

A man on a bus hears someone laugh.

Leave my title here.

•

My sight is dim, said a woman. Another must be singing.

I am sorry, the letter said, it is too soon for me to tell you about the paper train.

I mean, it is too soon for me to see you.

•

Birds are not designed for this space as in "The argument from design."

The letter said, a woman or man or boy can talk because paper fits into their hand.

The letter said the letter was looking for another address.

And, Thank you for touching my hair.

•

A woman or man or boy speaks but I see another talking.

To hear her is to make a reference to "The king who cannot project." A paper pomegranate.

The flames, for example, are snow. Someone else's example of red.

•

Thank you for the pomegranate.

A woman was touching my hair. Paper hair. The train is trying to hear.

The sun is someone else's voice. A particular kind of comb.

Paper birds, falling snow, a particular kind of boy.

•

She wants to trick the beginning into addressing itself again but I am still trying to project my voice.

Come here, triangle boy.

I am writing to comb myself, he writes. We never explain, sing the birds.

The letter began, Dear King Something. She explained the rest to her song.

•

Out of the bus and talking, he is trying to reappear. Her laugh is all around.

They think its echo will make a triangle. A sound between his hands.

Pieces of snow, falling apart. It is raining, explains the space.

Seeds in the ice, trying.

Thank the orange paper for trying. Paper flames in the snow.

A DIFFERENT HOUSE

Organs of the Projector

When the phone rings a man appears. His song rings and I am suddenly speaking to the true sun soloist. He is being a perfect listener or a void the perfect listener has stirred.

The organs of the projector are simple for him: "My statue has amplified its lungs." Without opening his eyes he has already moved back into the bad wheat. Snow flowers on his hands.

"This is not a painting," he says. "These are my clothes." In his fields the phone becomes the villain. "Do not look at the eagles," he says.

He cannot tell where one name begins and another falls away. His corridors collapse when the noon rain arrives. I do not look at the eagles.

The wires led to a hive

This is where I live but these are not my clothes. That is not my voice, a woman says.

She appears as herself. The same someone else.

Think of something quieter. Child-flower, bed-flower, the long pause her name created.

If a singer neglects her title long enough to lose her tone, the first of many eyes emerge.

This is the sign of a perfect listener. The look another not answering has.

A DIFFERENT HOUSE

When the conductor describes where she is, she feels no distress. "She has become still," says her throat. Moving, we see her film bending and everything reduces to the crushing tone of the triangle. (The film where she was born.)

She describes a hospital, but an organization can become sick too. She decides on a house instead. It has the quality of an expensive shadow. Each open window annexes a view, and the story takes its permits back. It says, beware the non-lethal ambulance.

In a loop of the perfect page, the film speaks and the conductor remains mute. This is a long pause, she says to herself. She moves between the parts of a blank. Do not call out the conductor's name. Do not repeat the perfect page.

The room is illuminated because the circulation of fluids is unequal. Try listening. Ding ding, a singer sings, but this is the conductor's performance. Try listening. Ding ding. (But think of a different house.)

This is an Accurate Picture of Space

A boy dressing himself in splashes.

The sand is smoke in the scene he comes in from. He erases the air around his mouth.

One name for a child is The Single Drop of Water. Another, The Sand a Single Drop Deflects.

His sound depends on a record skipping. The short song the sun repeats to itself.

A boy becomes related to water. A body recording over waves.

The tranquilized tongue

I didn't know I was asleep, said a man. Look! Opposite me from the other corner brushed one of his large eyes. There you are, he said. What I could see of him was wrapped in steam. His head seemed fastened under his chin. He opened his outer wrapper, which appeared to me large enough to put my arm down deep inside. His eyelids do not wake him. His reflection enlarges as it enters his eyes. Here, he lies down with a voice. Compared with his name, which exhausts itself, the fluid of the tranquilized tongue remains enclosed within a perfect circuit, and his troubled body opens without destroying the organs of address. It is certain he is one of a body of thousands.

A second silhouette

There is a woman and a boy or a man. One is standing behind a tree and speaking thinking. The speaker is singing This Is Not My Voice and A Train Is A Toy And Negative Rain. Inside the exposed song someone is hidden. The phonograph projects a second silhouette.

THIS IS A FILM ABOUT REAL TOY TRAINS

The actual overheard looking. That is not to say that looking is good and overhearing is bad, but that this is one way of having a tongue.

There is a simple, remembered charm about real toy tongues. What is wood is wood, what is cat is beautifully cast.

There is nothing self-conscious about a good, real boy. This is a film about real toy trees. The actual falling head.

That is not to say that light is good and tongues are bad, but that what is cast is embered in wood and this is one way of being conscious.

There is nothing simple about wood, being nothing but wires. Inside any good, real tongue there is another, beautifully cast. This is not to say there is nothing. There is wood, light, and wood.

This is a film about light, the boy said, failing to say that falling is good and wheat is what is overhead. That wire is the good one and that wire is the good one cast inside another dog.

The actual tongue is wood. Inside any real wheat is a bad tongue and welds. There is wood. That is one way of being burned.

The actual being that nothing falling is. Heat being nothing but heat. Any real wheat is nothing. That wire is the good wire and that wire is the good wire inside a bad tongue.

This is a film about the inside of trees. A boy saying I. That is one way of being overheard. Nothing is cast in wood and embers.

I KNOW THE LETTERS THIS WAY

The way I talk is a result of the way I hear her I was told but it took how long to show up in cursive. The small shapes I see when I close my eyes. That the waves are getting larger is one sign she is awake. I was born and then I learned to swim and then I learned how to pro-nounce the letters of the alphabet. I see her through them.

Do you want me to keep writing was the first thing I ever said or do you want me to stop. A man told me I would see him every other day and I did see he was a different man. I believed him to be otherwise. But since I knew the small shapes would not go away until I learned how to read I decided to talk to him anyway. There was a man whose name was a buckle and there was Mrs. Hand and Miss Toy. They were born when they learned how to swim.

To me it is like I am walking to a microphone. I do not know what it is I am like. Is it her I am talking to really. I am talking to someone I call by her name. I learned to swim so Miss Toy would not know how to pronounce me is also how I learned to read. How do I know there is going to be an accident. I can no longer speak with my hands. I would like to be called elsewhere.

When I chose where I was I was under her name. She herded my water to hers. I was missing said the woman who was missing. She said I got accident voice it is so obvious you are having a speaking accident and what would I like to call him. I learned to read with my hands by accident. We were letting them sleep she said. They say they let him say it the way I said it. With a name like that you are going to have accidents.

The microphone is waiting for someone I know I know. I know there is going to be an accident with my name. Buckle man says ding someone I know just learned how to read. It isn't enough for me to remember him now or something else she is like. I hear her hands are calling. They say ding. Or what it gloves.

It is so obvious I do not know what swimming means. Swimming obviously opens up something next to it. She feels so elsewhere and is. I saw a blank. Then waves. The way they alternate is leaving us again. It's a small ding. A letter I am thinking. They're gone. It's simple. We swim.

Do you want to hear my second sound is her shortest song. Have you seen this ring before. Buckle man says a toy hand is smaller than a full-sized finger. A tone beside another. They think they have seen my name before. It was here. It was here. We heard it. It was here before they started swimming. Look. We have similar streams.

A DISMANTLED MOUTH

Tuned droves

After an animal beacon sounds, a black disk masks whatever there is to see, three swallows enter a poplar's pulse, and the entire forest darkens a shade.

His illuminated ear

The new peacocks are known for speaking slowly in small, looping script. It is my duty to look away from their fluorescent beaks. They are ornamented with a bush of polished revolvers. "We are here to ensure that a letter enters your pocket." Complicating factors include the unconscious man's lapel and a swollen eye. The stillness of their feathers insist: "Here is a bed." As long as his body is encased in ice, the statue of his head remains consoled. The humming masked in an unfolding flower exposes the frozen observers to the slumped man's vertigo. If they fall to the side of his illuminated ear, his address will charge the walls: "I refuse to awaken." I refuse to close my swollen eye.

The convex vulture unearths ventricles

The vulture continually recovers but its chambers are no longer its own. Other barriers to circulation, such as the plural swan and its apprentice, the spoon, dissolve in separate spheres.

Vultures do not produce themselves. They produce paper. The vulture looks at the paper, then at the vulture. What vulture is made of suddenly curves.

The vulture reforms its hive by expanding its conception of paper. Everything that has formerly been paper is now protein.

Convex vultures have evolved in tandem with the helix owl because of real bees. The flesh of the helix owl is plagiarized and tough. It must be boiled while asleep when its tentacles are in full bloom.

The formation of paper occasionally exposes the encyclopedia pigeon to the statue fish. This introduction creates a failed (sterile) collage. Failed collages exhaust themselves in air, water, and air. They cannot communicate with one another because of a dense layer of salt. In order to remain above the surface they must be renamed.

Everything that vultures do not consume becomes surplus paper. A spawn occurs when there is a surplus of signals in the simple spine. Plural exhaust signals create a dense layer of paper as well as increased pigeon reception.

Boiling water creates a surplus of water. (The air the water is made of.) The formation of another dense layer of air causes new proteins to circulate.

The swan vulture never sleeps. It has evolved tentacles to keep itself conscious. The owl the vulture plagiarized remains moot. It cannot expose its flesh to the air.

His artificial wakefulness

That a subject can be stirred sixty feet from any open door, and that his reflection can only be seen from the bottom of a deep well reverses the bubbling forms from above.

Whatever water is torn from a single dismantled cube and its brotherly base is equally vibratory on the lips of the ventriloquist. He alone floods himself with cradles and corn.

Though two storm-soaked doves may replace the wind left by a palmful of palatial moths, without a properly placed mirror there can be no exit from his own cloaked corridors.

But what if another could clone the door? What if a bolt of cloth cones under his breast? Whoever rescinds a tangled carp from the most composite beast makes his severed silhouette visible again.

If the articles recessed in his flatness reappear, dust terns reproduce his score.

THE SONG OF STUNTED HAWKS

The singed horse doubles as an only swan. That their spawn's spores have become a seam between ions serves to re-divide its swells. Nurses mirage the song of stunted hawks by speaking out of phase with the queen. Warped by delusion, the arrow has always been part of a swarm. Atlantic transformations occur bilingually in the war between mice and frogs. Here, there are no neutral storms.

A DISMANTLED MOUTH

Because the helix owl's enlarger is not clock-like but revolves concentrically within, were I to uncoil its palate to extract an after-image its tones would smudge, owl-shaped, indefinitely.

Someone else answered the phone

Someone answered the phone first, because it was his duty, and at the window was a blue spotted salamander. I not only have to answer the second phone, the scarlet phone, but I have to look out the window all day.

Reptiles have a sign for "away" but it occurs only within amphibian phone range. When the phone rings again I am busy wasting the time of lizards and snakes. I do not give my name. I do not offer my water.

Where are you calling from? "The ocean and a building."

He asked if I wasn't perhaps polishing my own profile.

"That's the trouble. I'm not myself, although I am still on the clock," answered the man.

The ornate kingsnake was bored by my answer.

He said, "If you do not give up, I will not only answer the phone, but I will pause a long time before I speak."

It is my duty to look out the window until the phone rings again.

Looking at the scarlet phone, he thinks to himself, "Perhaps I, too, am in the ocean."

His name created a long pause.

Reptiles have a phone that rings once a day, for a long time, but it can only call the ocean.

"That's his name," he thinks to himself. "That's the long pause I created at the window."

I am still in the ocean but when the reptile phone rings again I can go back on the clock. I can go back to my building.

THE EMERGENCE OF A WOLF

The bee's stinger is like an enclosed, dark tongue. The atonal tortoise is a kind of dictionary in reverse. To see them is to feel one's teeth become abstract. They survive as obstacles to grammar and song. They do not, then, accept the vibrations in an ear, for example, as proof of sound. The drama of their wavelengths occurs just before the emergence of a wolf. The phonological limbs of bees are evident on the plains of an impossible sentence. Its dance, similarly, organizes eagles into the habits that constitute captivity. These are the elements of a frozen brook.

THE CONTINUOUS CORNER

Box normal.

Box normal, okay?

Miss was just around the corner and I knew she could hear the sound our hands hid. Ding tried to box normal but both bees opened anyway.

Wake up, little what, wake up and be still.

Miss said I should not speak because a bee is clearing its wings. This made an image, for a time. And if I did, I would wake up without a throat.

Ding put both bees back and my ears got clear. I woke up a little. Miss put a page in my throat because it was not yet a story.

Wake up a little more, Ding. Be still, and hear a bee breathing.

•

My silence had been long enough for the room to reappear. I decided to play "flag" on both pianos. Ding preserved the sound of a tiny hive.

Whose house is this, with Halloween wine and dark crackers? we wondered. Miss wondered too, but as an adult does, with real wine and lighter crackers.

"flag" is a game for one player. It begins when two adult vines enter the room. The fourth and fifth players hold still for various intervals of time, closing their eyes. All involved divide into thirds until the nest becomes neat.

There is no such thing as bee's blood. Try telling that to my throat.

•

These I knew, even in the dark, by hand, but when I woke into the room the ceiling lowered, and the blooms did not want to play their parts.

Purpose mirrors are real but I wondered how the big hive sounds.

Hello. Normal Hello.

The room held together somehow despite the vibrations of a non-standard greeting.

Would I be allowed to walk around the continuous corner?

The blooms grew large and blocked my path. Normal Hello.

Had I missed the turning of feet? If I had it had certainly happened suddenly, quickly, during the strong pause my name created. But since the corner was still in the room I decided to walk. My head lowered. My path lowered. The continuous corner remained a sill.

•

The paper path bloomed and rose toned bulbs corrected our steps. A cloud and a code, crossing.

The mandatory distance from the non-lethal ambulance is one hundred solid digits. Keep that in mind. The minimum time for hive transfers is half of half that. And, only half of that beep is sustainable.

Be still. Do not discuss the continuous corner.

We had not yet acknowledged the distance but I could feel the blooms bowing. What I wished for was what Miss had walked towards from a great distance. Closing in is its own reward.

A boom does not belong. I remember that much. A boom does not belong and neither does its inverse. Rather, an analog awaits. This is not an ambush, as an ambush implies a corner and vines.

Ding boomed backwards. That is why her songs beep.

•

I remember being explicit. I said, I am being explicit, but my not-body had incompletely accrued.

No adult vines allowed. I believed it and in believing it the sign that told me to remain blank grew bewildered.

Rose schools allow implicit followers to bunk excess water. I am allowed to transfer new water to any closed hive. However, if I begin to believe any of the signs surrounding the vines I am supposed to hover above the rain.

The language of vines is inherently explicit. Keep that in mind during an ambush.

•

The determiner hums to denote its hide. Keep that in mind during transfers. Whatever water is not collected expands the vocabulary of vines:

I like your hide.

No, I like *your* hide.

•

The determiner knows that ants are not a symptom: I am sorry, Miss, but they're not coming up on the screen. That's like asking what the most important part of the floor is. I mean, I could pretend that ants are a symptom, and give you a small shovel, but that would be a false address.

If I think up a signature large enough for all the essential paper then sure, I'll let you know. Conversely, if the opposite happens I'll remain silent. Because the core of any sonar is silence, if the opposite happens, believe me, you'll never hear your name.

•

Miss wants more Halloween wine but the path is growing dark. Boom boom beep. I am posing in the rain while the altitude expands.

Miss is posing too but it takes her longer to wind. Winding is not easy on a path grown dark. Miss is walking from a great distance. It seems pretty great, from here.

•

We always proceed from a rigid mouth and a closed star. More than the dawn, for someone else to find our edges was the main thing. Who flung to me, who flung to Miss, who flung went translated to regions of exactness.

Exactly, said the determiner: We help our songs to die.

We worked early and late, patiently and hard. We wrote a story, which was lit, like this, from within, though from a different source.

The blooms do not last long when they leave the outside. In this spectrum, they live inside a rain system, where they think themselves able to confer a natural redness, the perfect red of their clapping hands.

Blend with the tree-tops, Ding, the room apprehends us all.

•

The determiner explains: "flag" is a game in four parts. It consists of picking up any object in the room and saying "flag" loudly. If an actual flag is encountered, the flag is held in the right hand, lowered slowly, and the speaker creates a strong pause.

Here, think of who is in the room, eavesdropping.

•

Miss does not notice the fireworks, Ding always sways, and the perfect page retreats.

It says: The language of flags is not sustainable.

Please do not call me honey. Please do not repeat the perfect page.

Instead of describing the room, Miss chooses to sing "Instead."

Ding remembers being opposed. She thinks, I am being opposed. Yet this mention is less narration than the hour where all her work goes.

·

Because I have a neat nest and a phonetic head, Miss allows me to feed the bees.

Instead of describing the language of bees, I have chosen to turn their flags into a phone. An infusion of fur into the grafting emulsion allows a message to dip into view:

We have been (burned) discovered.

Look, I do not say, to my body. In its place I say I am trying to demonstrate that we live in a non-tragic universe.

Hello? (Normal silence.) Hold the flag still.

·

The page in my throat won't go away. I know that ants are not a symptom, but I have chosen to transfer my water today.

Miss says I am allowed to play eat a piece of the toy piano's peel.

The determiner found my not-body but it was too immature to claim: There is harm in the boy, but never thought.

I thought, I am clotting like a monument in soda water.

·

Bee's blood contains two non-lethal booms: This is an expansive shadow, and, This has been a long pause.

The vines never thought I would deny the perfect page. Purpose mirrors silence. That is what they say.

Ding boxes normal. Adult vines dissolve. The continuous corner is coming near. Flags are not a symptom of "flag" the determiner wants me to say. The blooms re-live the continuous corner in part of the perfect page.

•

Because we are no longer covered in vines Miss thinks the opposite happened. The determiner echoes the blooms:

Animal flag. Ambulance flag. The perfect flag in a negative box.

The continuous corner describes itself. It says: Do not look at the fireworks, and, Our songs are dying much too slow.

Wake up, little image, an ambush awaits.

Believe me, fellow flags, these booms will never beep.

A DING AND ITS ECHO

Inside Any Good Song Someone Is Lost

There is a splash. There is another splash. There is another. There is a man a man two women a boy and a boy. Something else. Someone else. I can't see past the wheat and birds I can't see. There is a singer. Is there a second singer? There is. That is, you can record yourself from the center of a parade. The clouds are large. You are little and the clouds are so large.

A DISTANT ADDRESS

A boy suspects he has been exhumed, ever since his shadows had grown in number, ever since it was announced that "Subjects will no longer reside under the sun but in the ghost it represents." Whoever does not avert their eyes from this false eclipse listens to a bloodstream in reverse. Perhaps he will become more common when the negative mouth is active again, and in this formation, a distant address.

WITHOUT MY LETTERS

In their natural condition, my letters appear near but remote.

"When you hear the higher tone, a boy becomes apparent" traced in the writing of another's hand.

His artificial wakefulness is the true subject.

•

When the work was finished, there were no chapters.

The name of the child was It Is Not Here.

It is unlikely this is precise.

To reproduce his mother's voice, hydrogen was added to the body.

For all this activity, the sound was flat.

•

He is suddenly working.

"Today I want to tell you where you are."

Moving the cards, the whole thing turns over.

His statue deteriorates. The shoulders, the long, slender arms.

•

He appears to himself as the arrival of waves.

I must wait, completely still, without my letters.

•

Now the script suggests still waters. The scene of a lamp, not lit.

It begins: "In the sky, when I was a child."

His lungs have filled again.

•

"It's raining." It's raining.

When you read the body of water inside him, another is singing to me.

Small fires in the desert

The double-tongued music emerges first in the "o" of the machine. All other letters have been omitted. Its inverted body splits, becomes a faithful shadow, when its enveloped organs activate a pattern. (Small fires in the desert.)

An echoed exoskeleton

A man reflecting snakes is covered in patterns. This is not another language but two treatments of the same tongue. There is very little "place" left inside him afterward. His segments seem to circle an absence. Because they resemble stars an eruption of memory re-shapes the supple scales of the abandoned skin subsequently replaced by his face. Spasms in his stomach occur to interrupt the absorption of stones. Elsewhere, the sun rephrases a tree.

It is relatively easy to stop saying "I" when the revolving stories of his host reappear. For example, a delirious musician who replays, randomizes or slivers everything he hears has discovered vestiges of human or animal "bones" in the REM movements of babies. In this case, the nest is acoustic in nature. The parts of his score form a corral of previously transparent sights. Unacknowledged iron is used to flatten the surface, to make reference to the materials of the synchronized swords dividing his pages.

These sacrificial words form a feigned body which evades him during sleep. (This is how captivity by flower takes shape.) Here, a song characterizes itself by trying to connect to its fields. As part of the process, his second body develops a prophylactic screen in which the speaking person and his organs are not in consensus. The development of the solar system is no longer a suitable theme because the sedimentary ostrich, at this precise moment, becomes a force of predation to him. Its multiplying tails require a series of ruptures between the solarized "I" and the voice he reveals to the perfect listener.

WAITING FOR MY NAME

The sound hit her hand in tiny waves.

Each one as it is.

The current picked up between the thumb and forefinger, through the same subtle channels.

·

Having reached an immense swell, I said perhaps it is true the sentence was: She sang the solo portions. He returned the skull to its place.

·

There's an old face near the real, visible action.

The rest of the night is related to its song.

·

Tiny waves progress from a skull.

Remembering is when this does not happen.

·

The sound shapes itself and, on the appointed day, if nothing is alone, I know nothing, so that I, too, have come back.

·

A gesture of the hand. The sound in a story.

Me, near the beginning, waiting for my name.

·

The drift between such deserts is one reason for instinct.

When I write her name is a secret name, the wax removed lets something tumble over me from the air.

•

Alone, speaking sometimes with a slight curvature, I would like to know I will wake up there, so I can observe myself. Or at least the lower hemispheres.

A DING AND ITS ECHO

I think a boy is a hive, says a woman.

She hears a bus and a boy is blotted.

The birds are here. I hear them.

They want me to keep on writing, "I walked until the letters swelled"
but I think a boy is a ray, an anything tree.

He strays through Not Here, she says. I am starting to hear him in
waves.

I am not her son. A ding and its echo, snow.

The same subtle music emerges elsewhere.

She is starting to seed the ice with waves. The sequence is precise.

The final hands count beginning sounds.

I understood, "I am writing until my tracings move" even without the
birds.

Her laugh is a triangle.

My voice is a reference to almost nothing.

"He wants to arrive in waves" was a space he had made by asking
himself a question.

I woke up there, redundant as snow.

THE FORMATION OF FLOWERS

When a phonograph and a projector converge, they conceive two distinct components: echoes and antennae. This is a new relationship dubbed with a beautiful glyph ("The formation of flowers"). From the beginning, the radiator of vibrations and images portrays a struggle between resonance and digression. The battle takes place in double-voiced prose. The aim is to evenly divide the crude curve of circulation.

First, white gloves are placed on the machinery. A throat flute organizes the exterior into a full spectrum of mimetic polyalloys. Finally, two tape heads record the participants from equidistant outposts. (Please keep in mind that phonological species, like feral animals, are interrelated through a series of musical networks.)

If one of the opponents displays an opaque residue after the first meeting, a rudimentary branch dissolves to help the audience observe. However, if the performance culminates in the production of an irregularly shaped vowel the final episode coincides with simultaneous self-immolation. Upon completion, their respective widows are presented with gathered kindling one might (but must not) torch.

WHENEVER THE TWOS REPRODUCE

He listens when I hear myself. We both arrived in rain.

There was the learning to read accident. The remember who accident. Small tones we no longer speak to ourselves.

•

"We no longer need you to seal yourself in signals," said the one I believed away.

I would like to ask but I don't speak buckle. He said this by folding his arms.

•

There was a question, an ear. The flat stones beside me.

I call the body of water inside him Whenever the Twos Reproduce.

•

A wake in the stream of subjects, this is the way it left us talking.

"The story of leaving begins with A." "Whenever I see him, he hears a child."

•

His voice corresponds with the body it extends.

The one who tells me I heard the feathers fall.

They Showed a Film of Walking to Water

A woman walking beside me. She hears bees when she swims was the title. The scene folds out from the flat stone the sun is.

I am watching her trace the air where I was but they want me to see something else, her water double, a paper palace, but I am on a bus again.

She was folding her arms to make a mirage, touching the snow in a sentence. She knows I know I will disappear tonight, a time-lapsed splash in my place.

Inside any good song is a small piece of snow is the one I am listening for.

ORANGE WATER

The bloom. The boiling water. Bees. Real flowers release bees. Real flowers bloom orange. Real bees bloom in boiling water. Real water releases bees. Boiling real bees releases flowers. The flowers bloom. The bees bloom. The water blooms. The boiling blooms. Real flowers. Real bees. Real water. Flowers are not real. Bees are not real. Water is not real. Release the bees. Boil the bees. Water the bees. Real water. Orange flowers. Orange water.